SPEED-READ FOR VIOL

VELOCITY, AGILITY & CONCENTRATION DRILLS

MB21780

BY JOHN BAUER

BILL'S MUSIC SHELF

Preface

In language, speed reading relies on eye focus, mental focus, and seeing groups of letters, or groups of words, as units. The same priciples apply to music reading.

This book is designed to develop those abilities.

The Appendix gives a detailed guide for how to use the book to develop the 'focus' technics. The recommended procedures take about 15-25 minutes to practice one entry. After one month it is typical for a person to improve 45%. For example: If a person can read a new entry at an mm. setting of 72, one will increase the initial speed to about 104 in one month.

Practicing all of the entries as designed will result in all possible finger patterns being covered, and in all possible combinations of whole steps and half steps.

Table of Contents

The Drills

Eventually patterns 1-24 should be practiced in the Major key signatures of C, D, E, F, whole tones, and in semi-tones. Triplets are for augmented seconds.

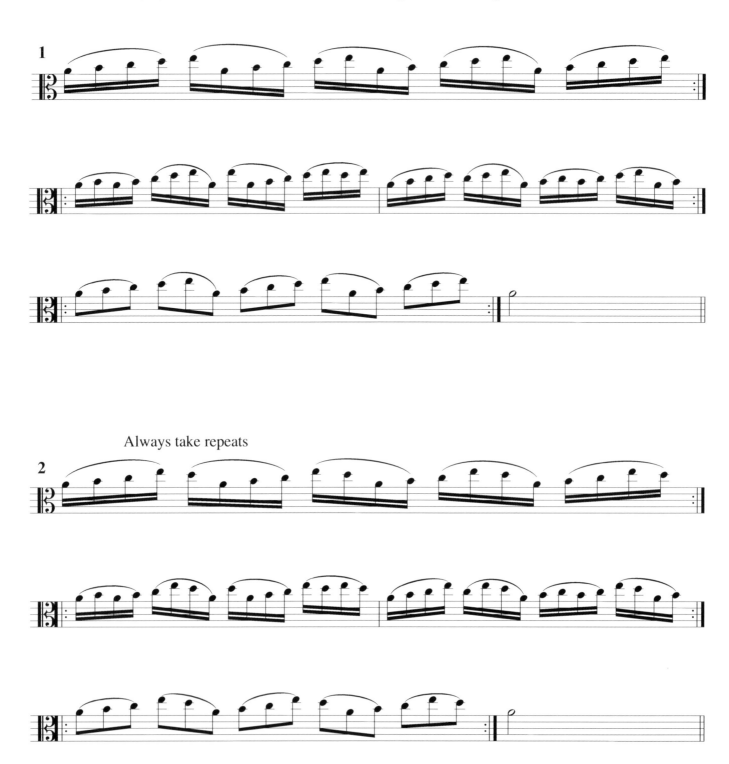

Always take repeats

Ear training: use automatic chromatic tuner on first line

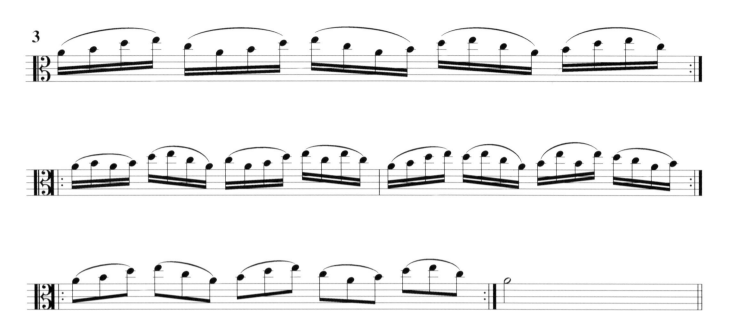

Focus energy in the left fingers...quiet left hand.

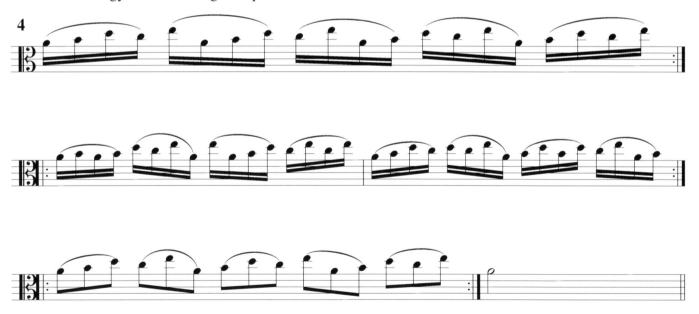

Easy attitude

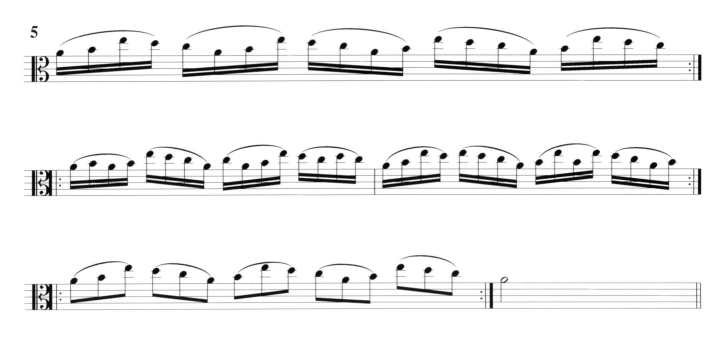

Retain fingers. See line 2. Apply principle throughout.

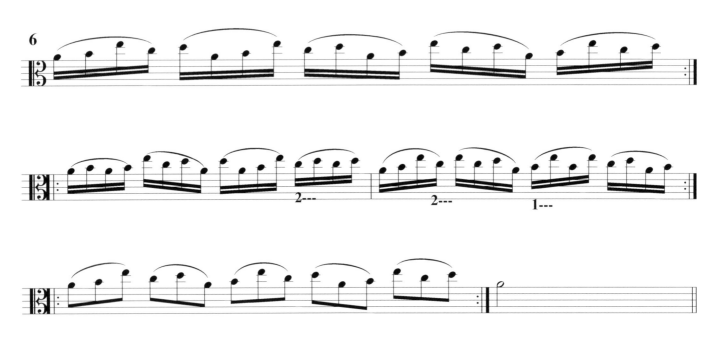

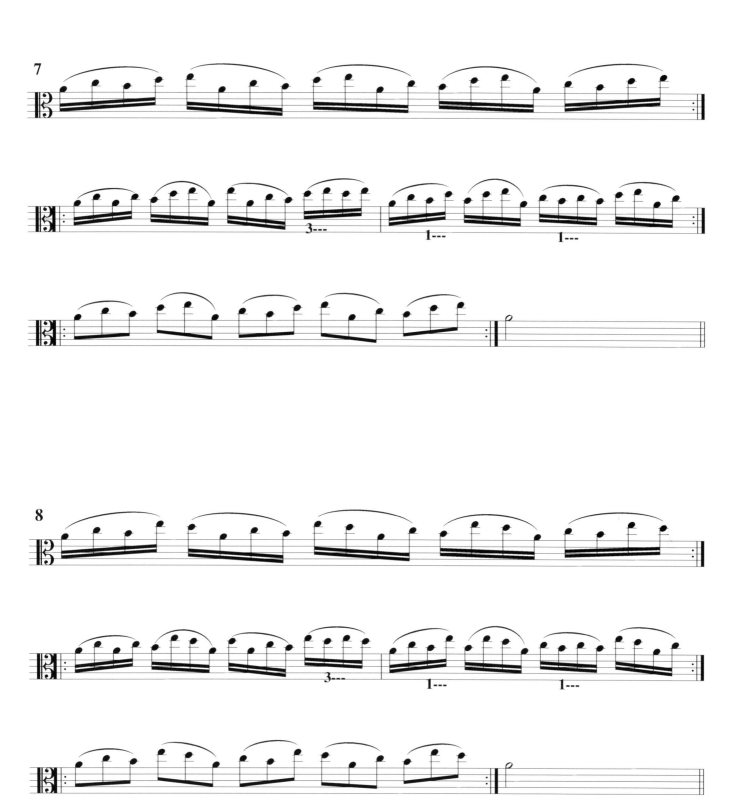

9

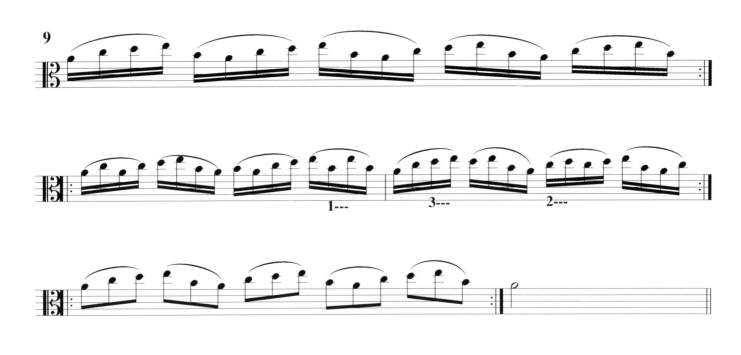

Check left thumb placement

10

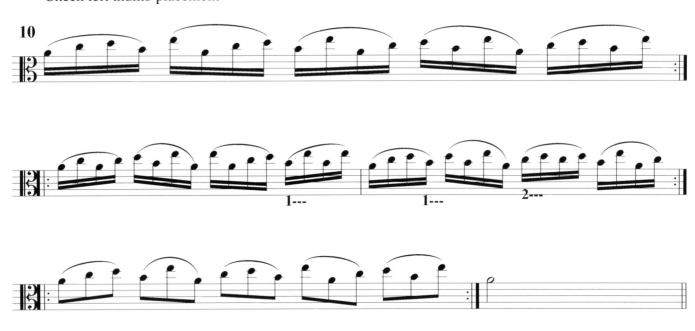

"Slap" fingers of the left hand, without tension.

13

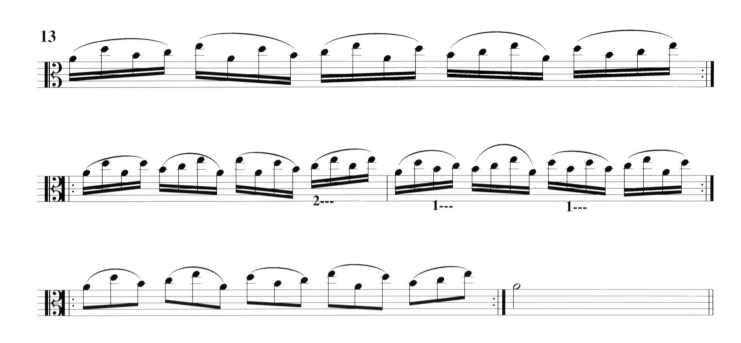

Slap high fourth finger.

14

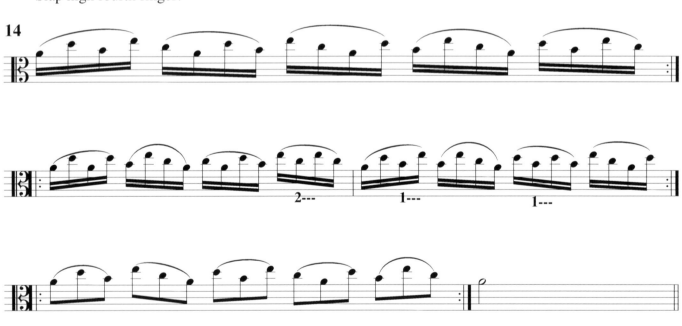

Anticipating finger placement is an element of efficiency.

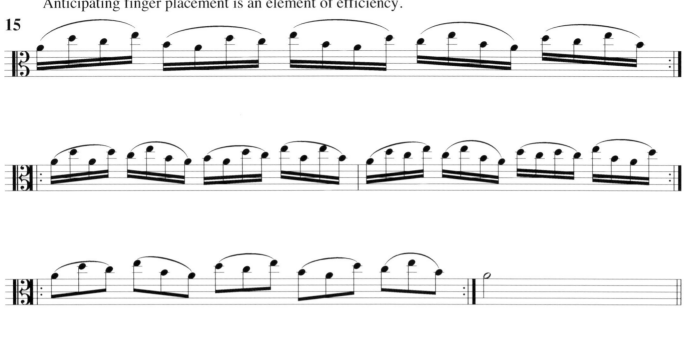

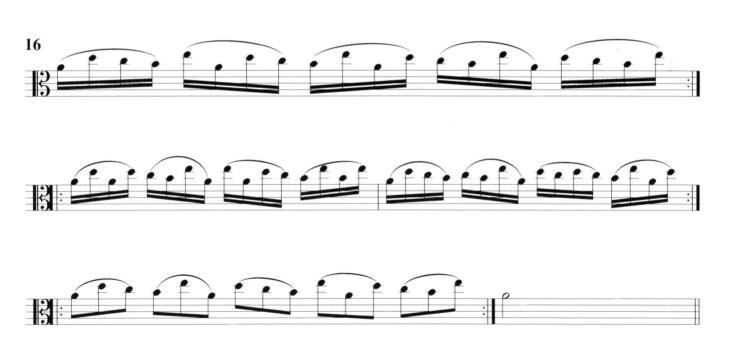

17

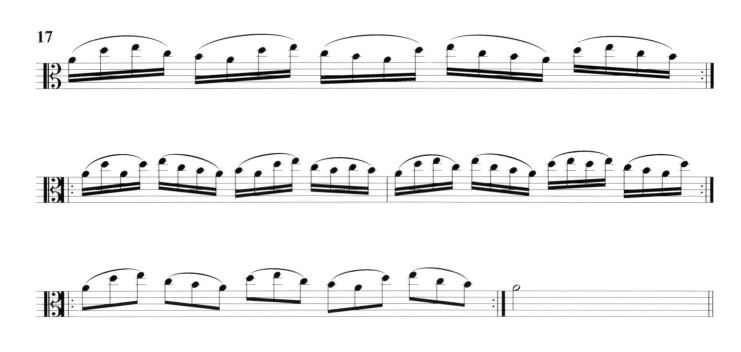

Retain fingers. See line 2. Apply principle throughout.

18

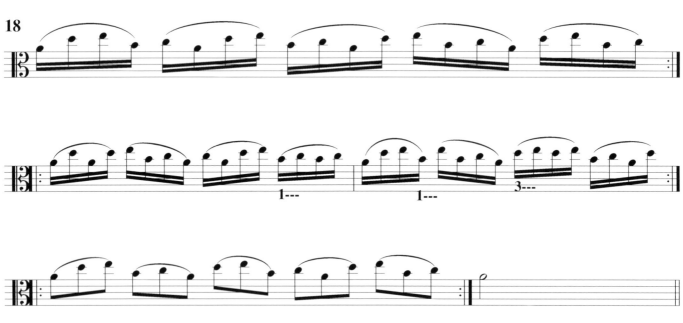

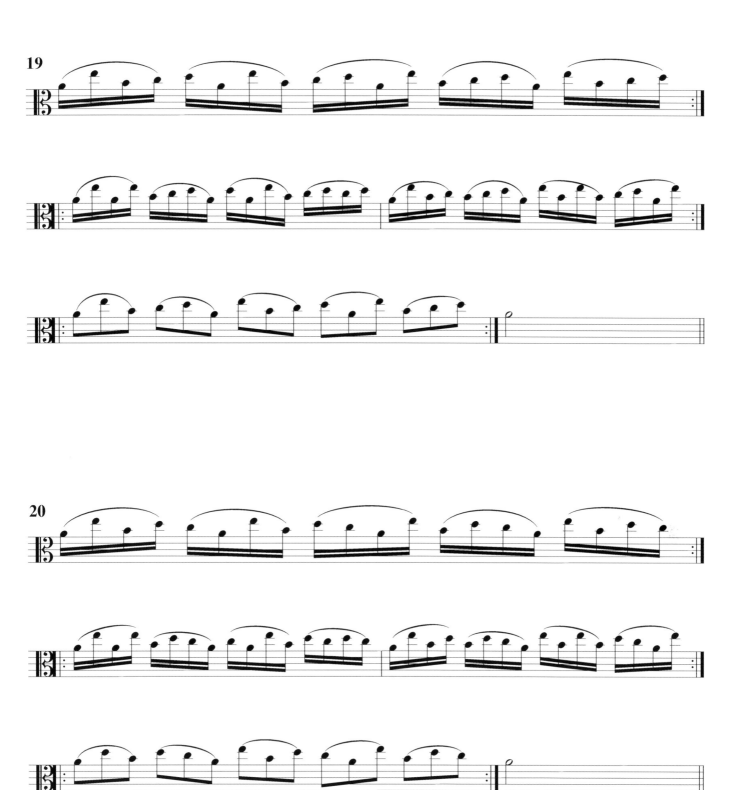

Focus energy in left fingers...quiet hand.

Slap high fourth finger.

Easy attitude

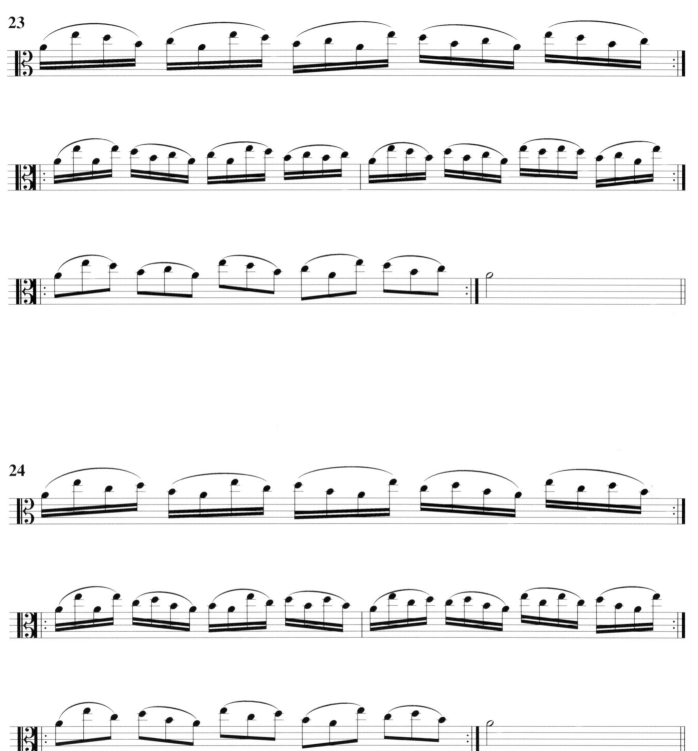

Eventually patterns 25-48 should be practiced in the Major key signatures of F, G, A, B flat, whole tones and in semi-tones. Triplets are for augmented seconds.

25

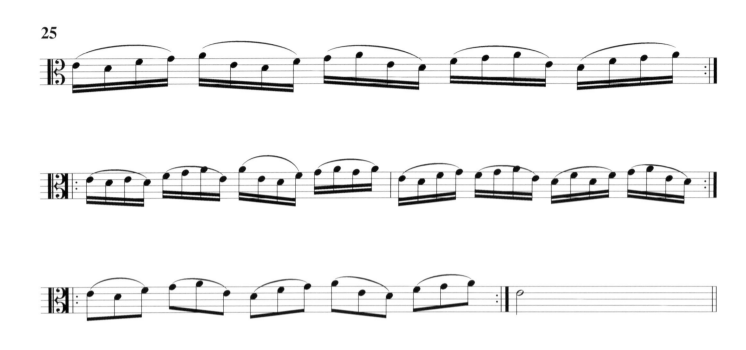

Notice left finger contact points...pads.

26

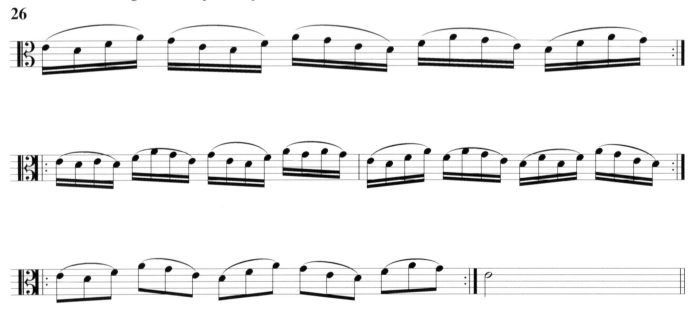

Left finger contact should be centered or a little to left side of string.

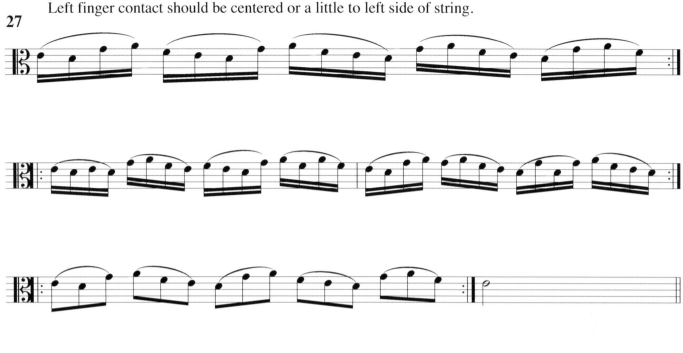

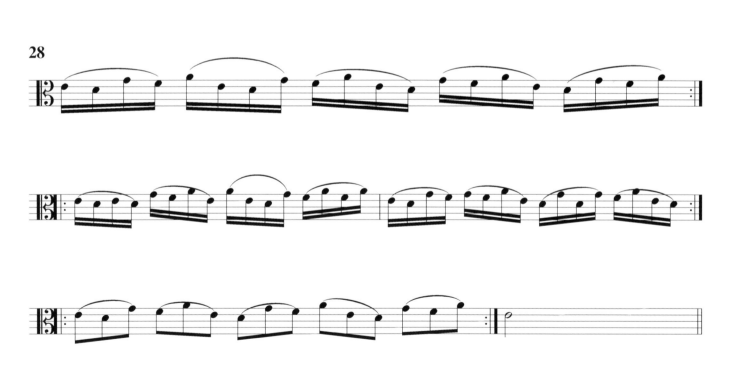

29

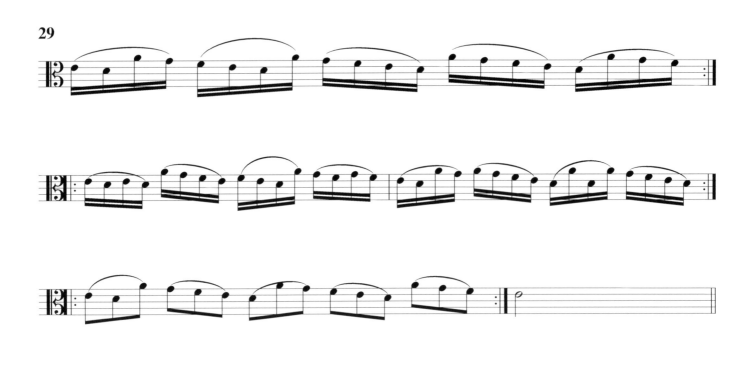

Always take repeats

30

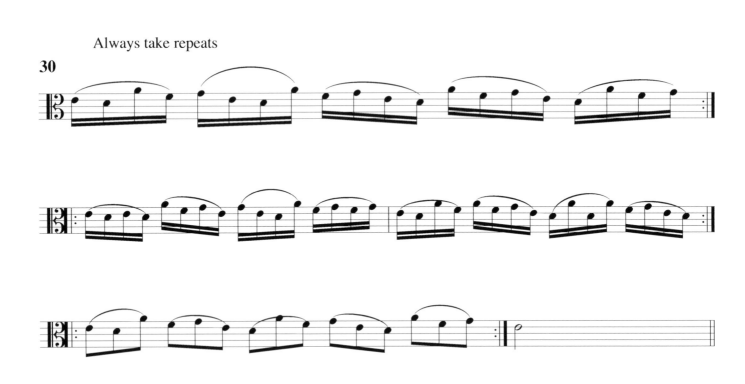

31

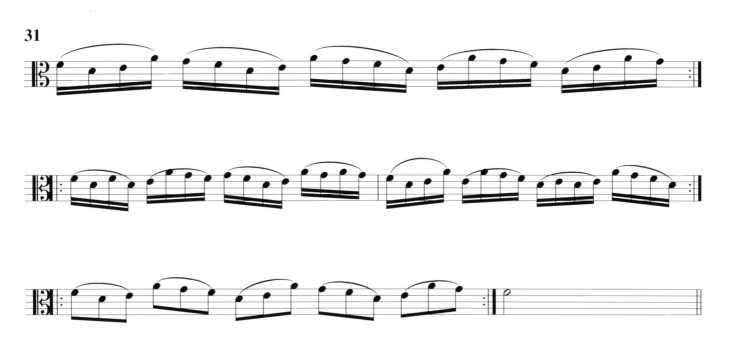

Check left thumb placement

32

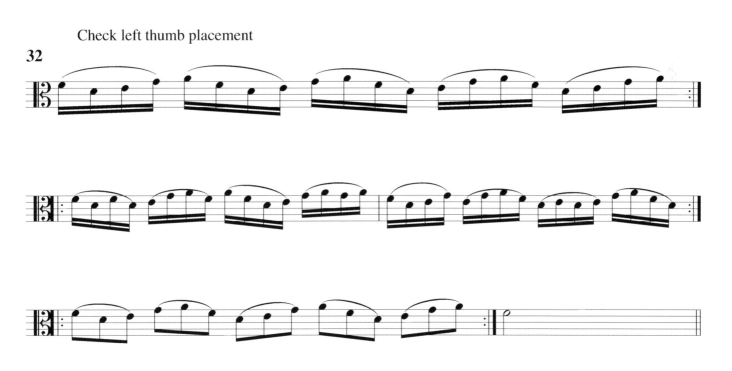

19

33

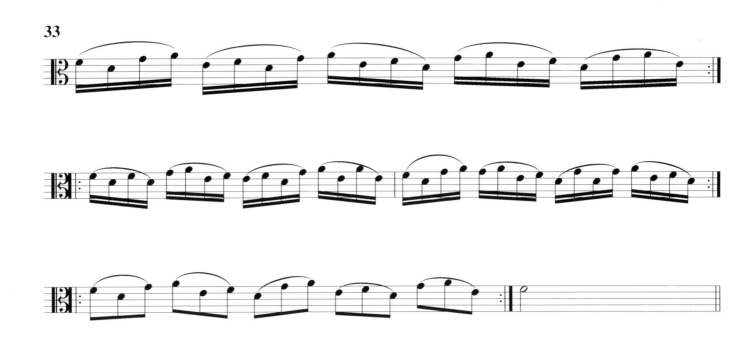

Keep idle fingers over string being played

34

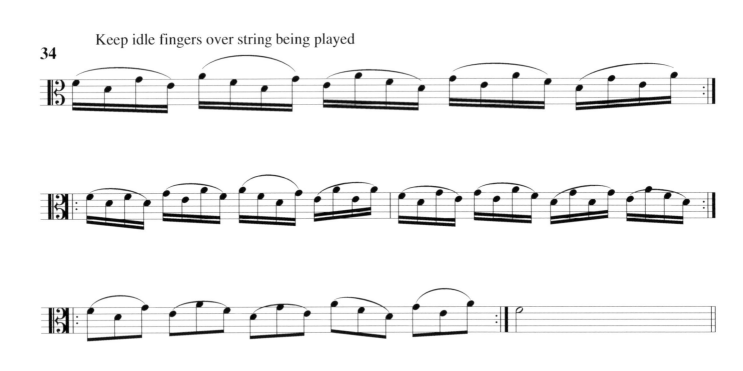

35

36

37

Easy attitude

38

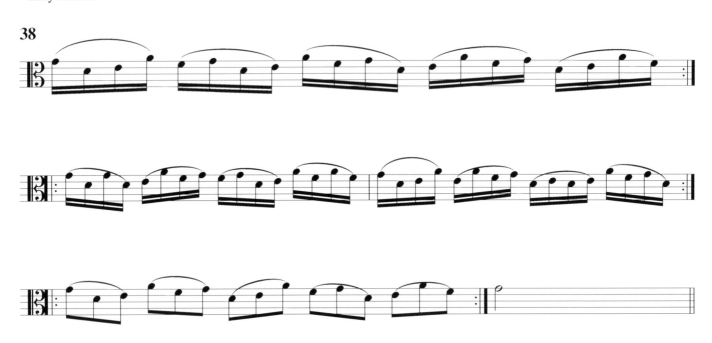

39

40

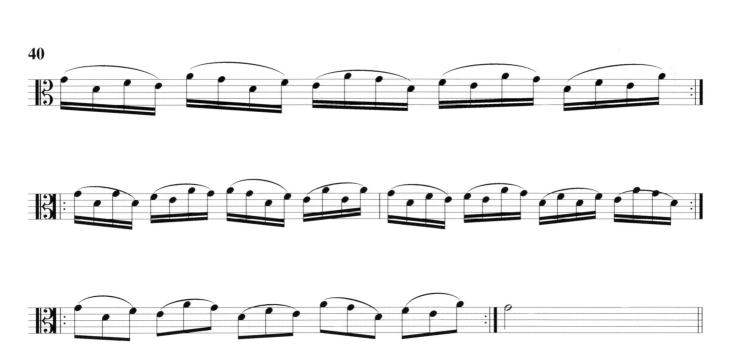

41

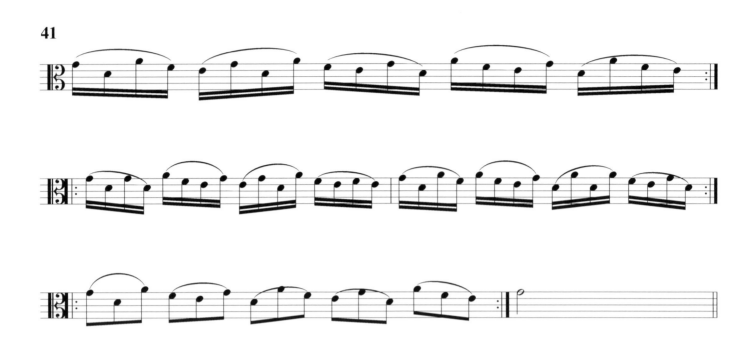

42

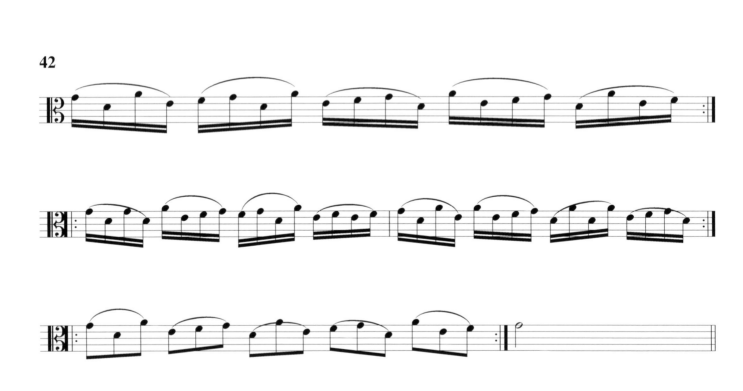

43

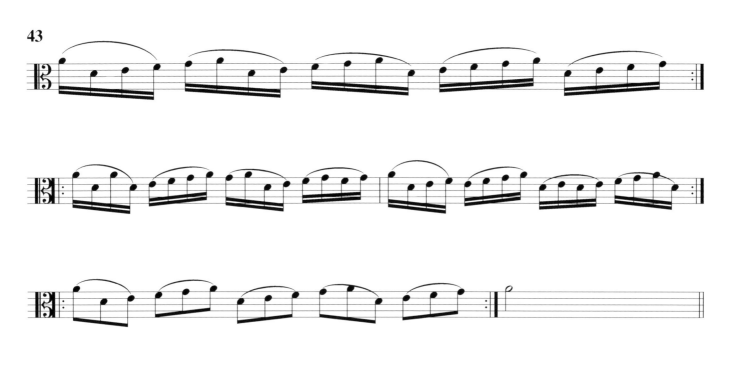

Always take repeats

44

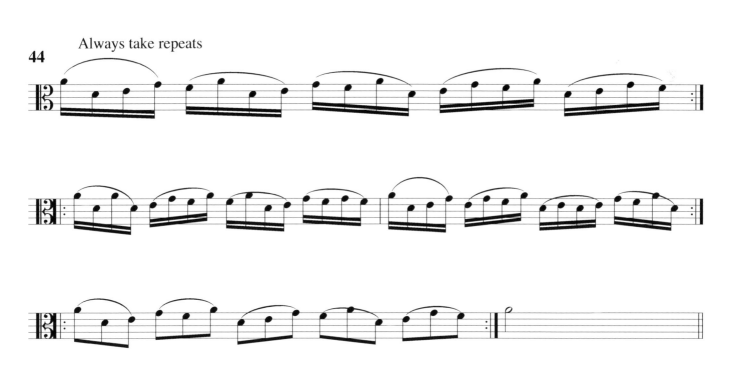

45

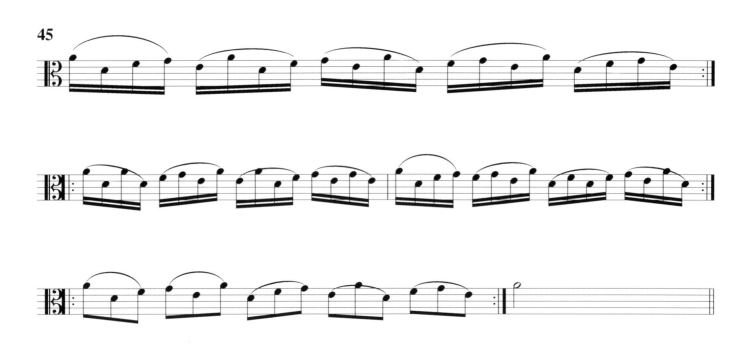

Keep idle fingers over string being played

46

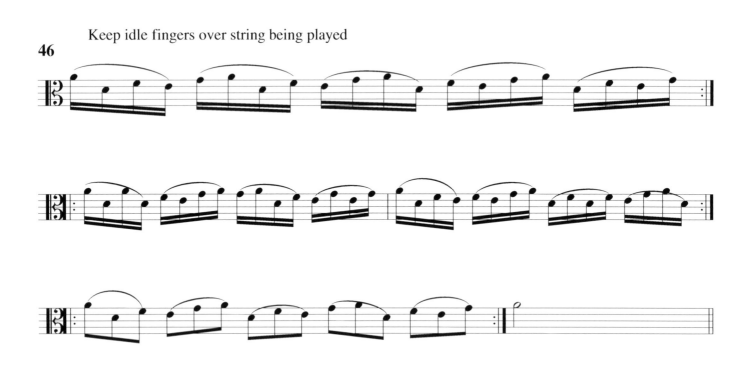

26

Easy attitude

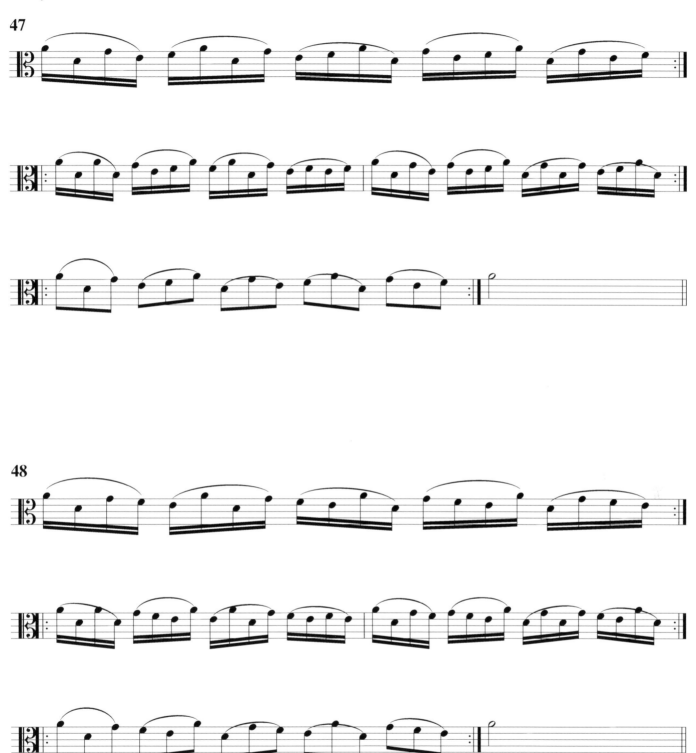

Eventually studies 49-72 should be practiced in the Major key signatures of B flat, C, D, E flat, whole tones, and half steps. Triplets are for augmented seconds.

49

50

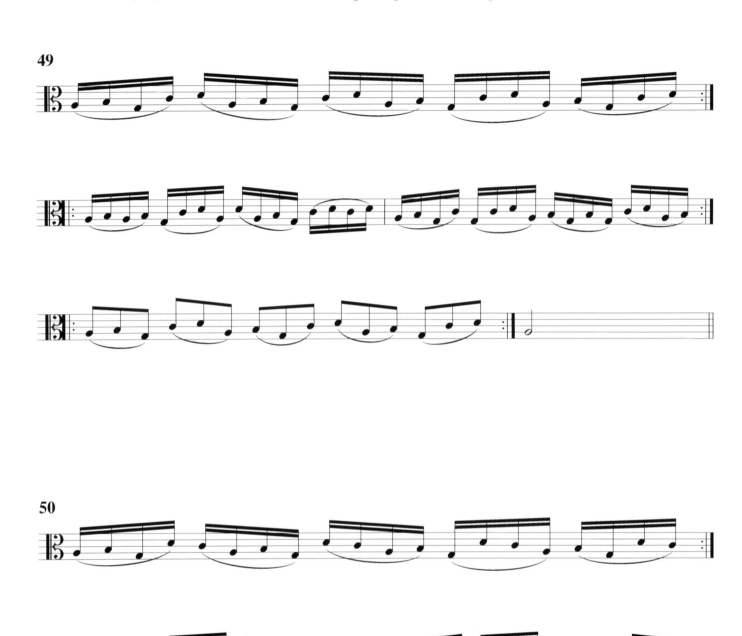

51

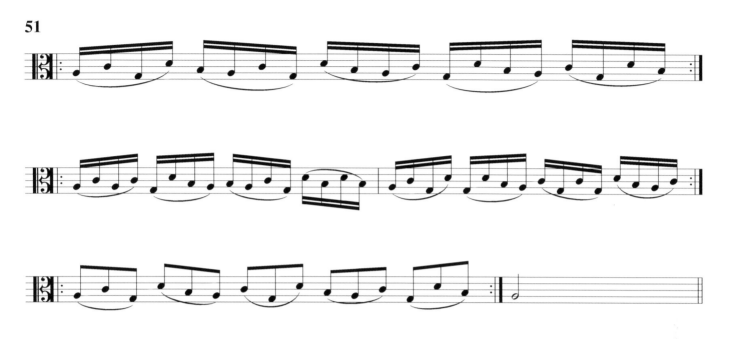

52

Always take repeats

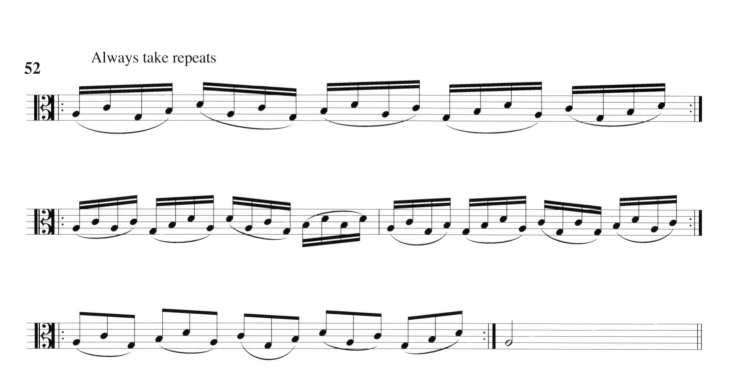

53

54

55

56

57

58

59

60

Check left thumb placement

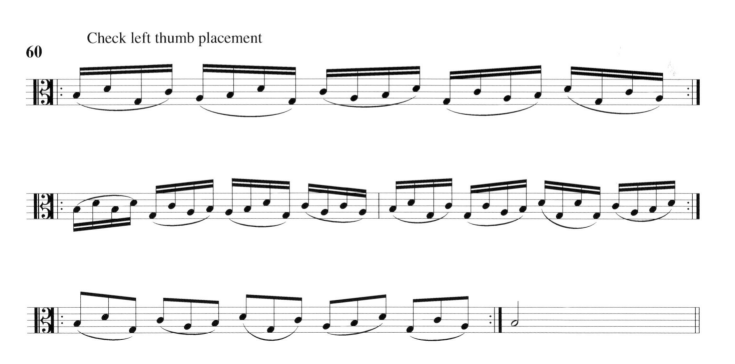

61

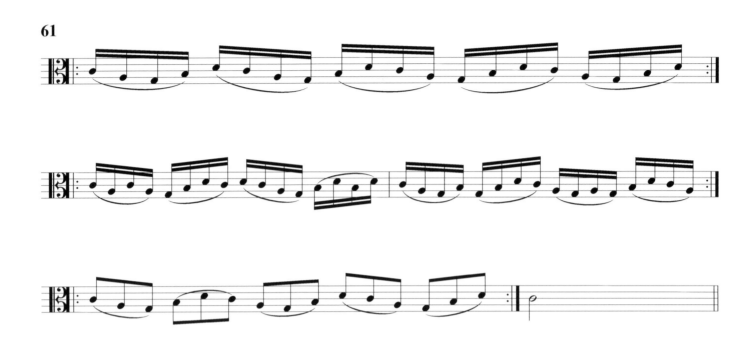

62

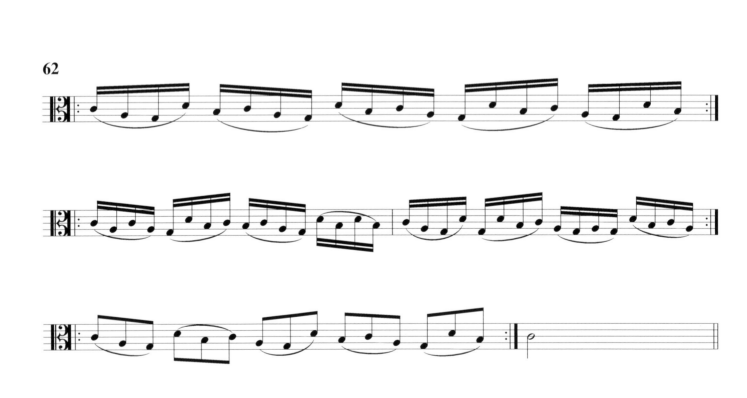

Easy attitude

63

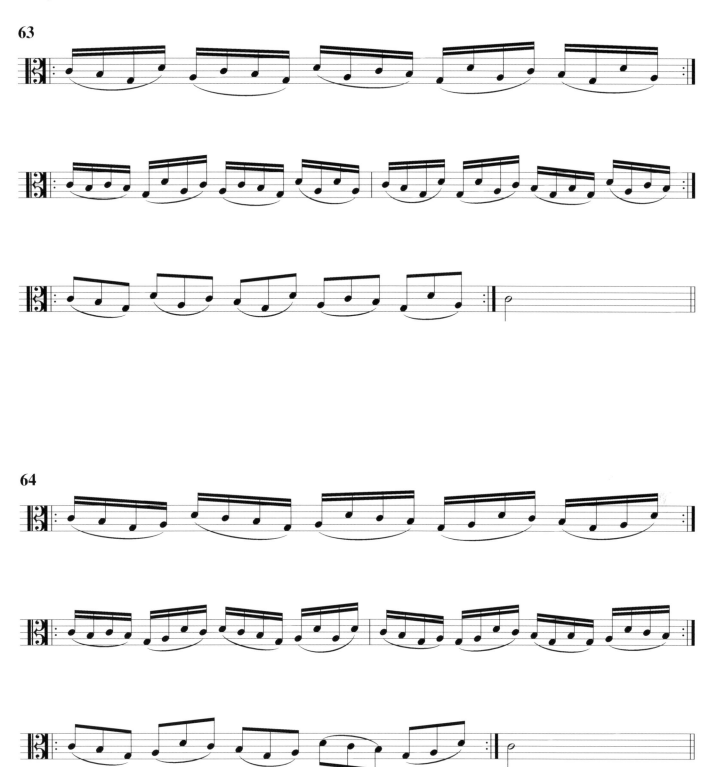

64

65

Keep idle fingers over string being played

66

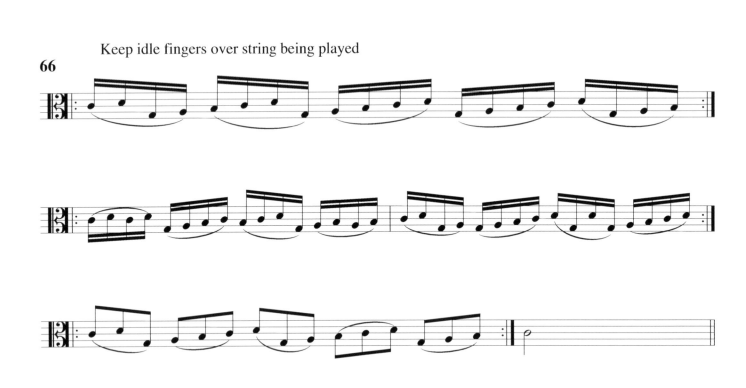

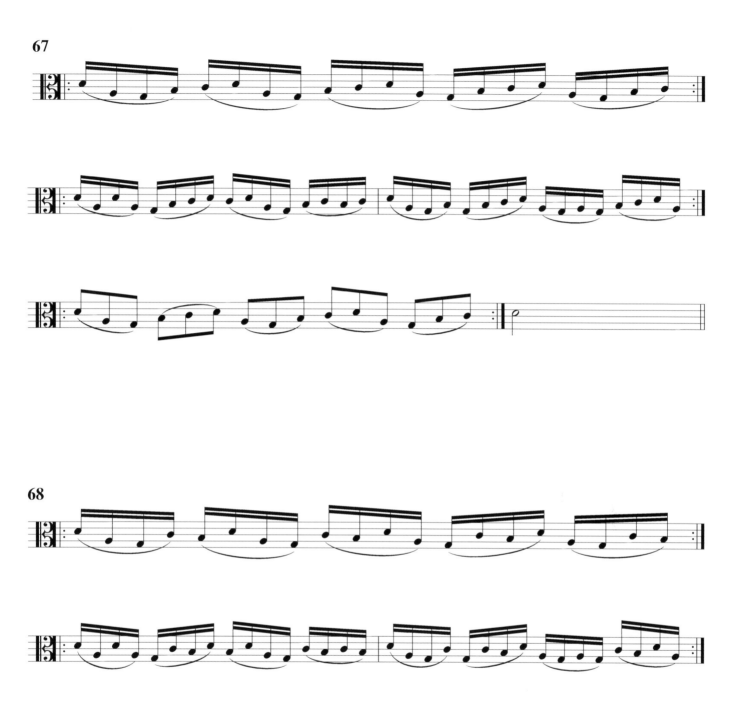

69

70

71

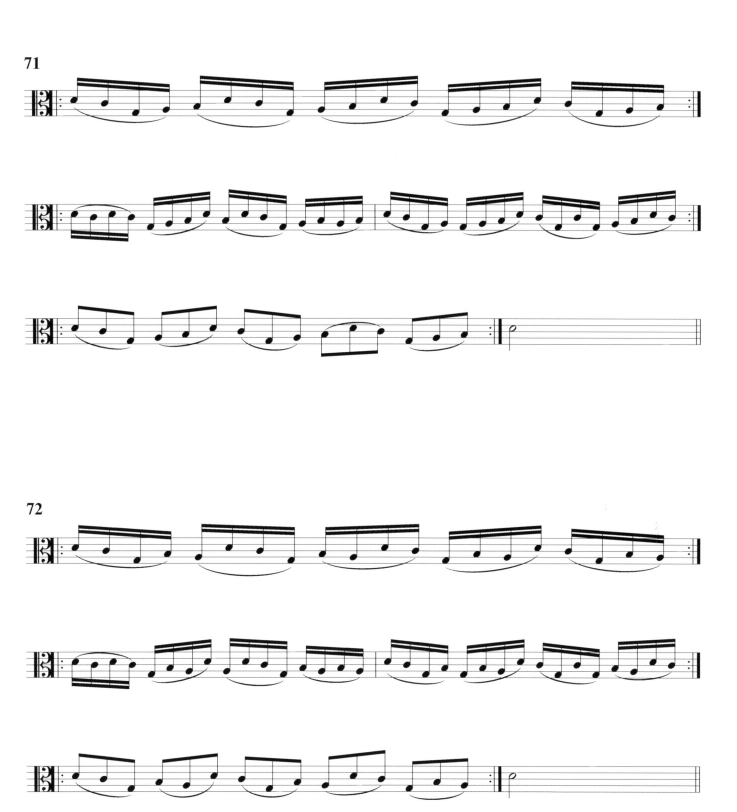

72

Eventually patterns 73-96 should be practiced in the Major key signatures of B, D, A, E, whole tones and in semi-tones. Triplets are for augmented seconds.

73

Always take repeats

74

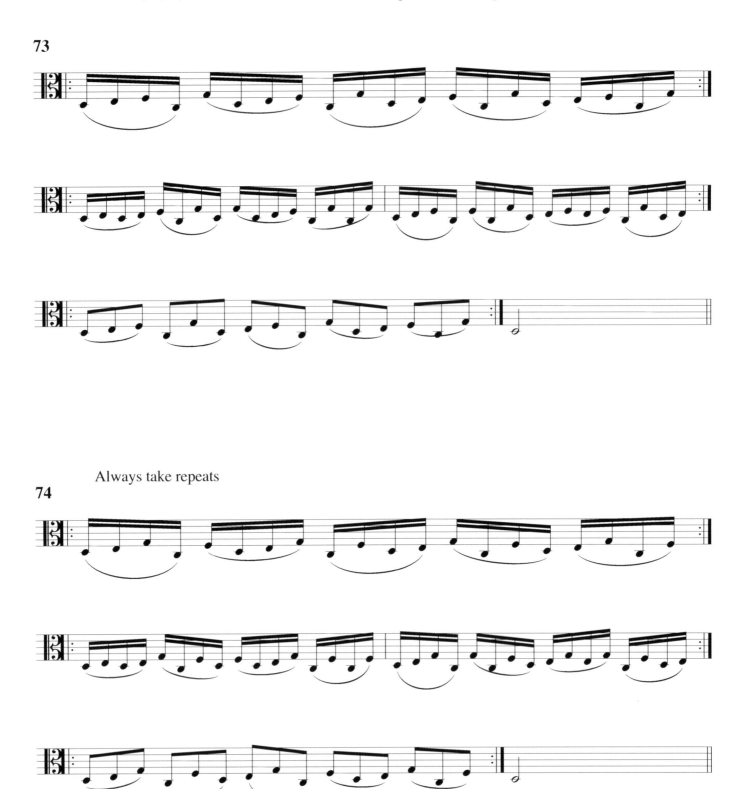

75

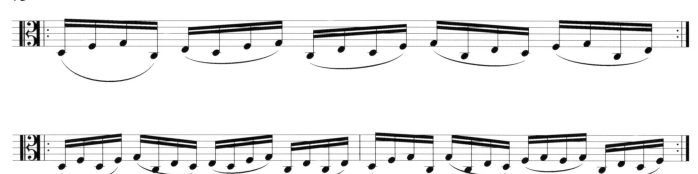

76

77

78

79

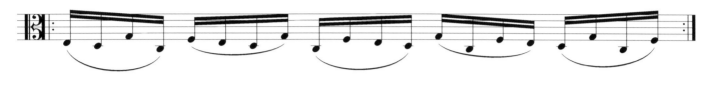

80

81

Keep idle fingers over string being played

82

Easy attitude

83

84

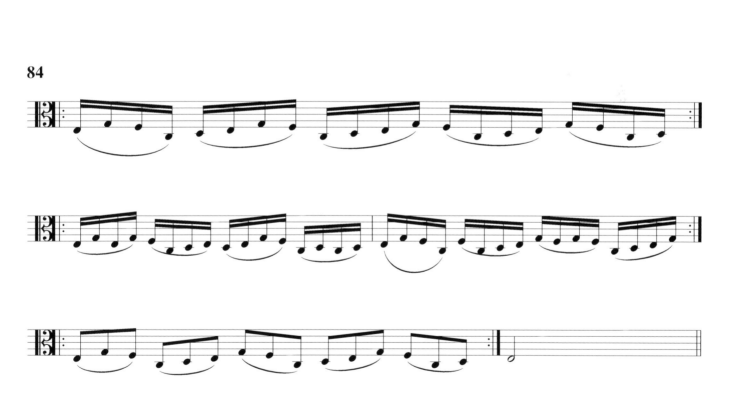

85

86

87

Check left thumb placement

88

89

Focus energy in left fingers

90

91

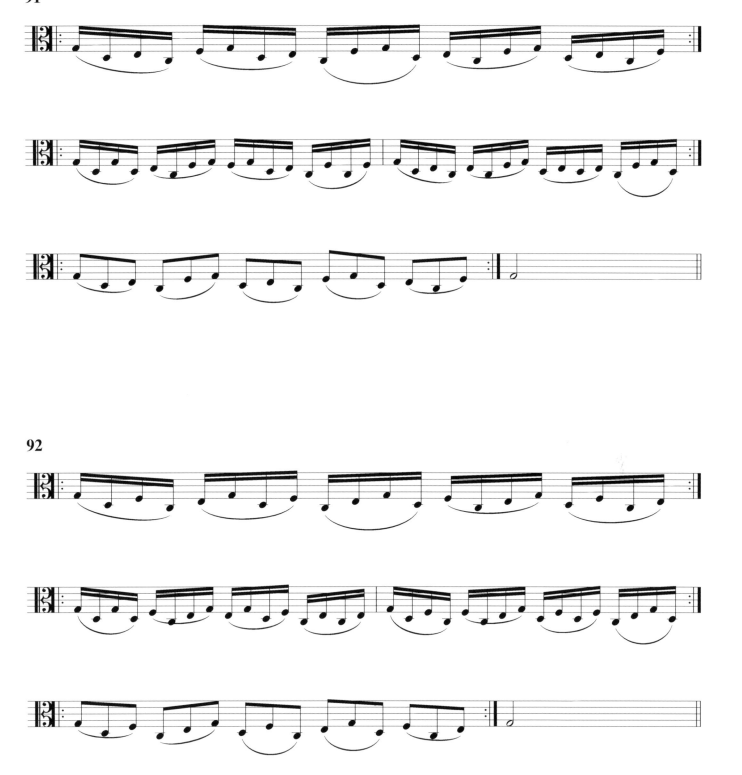

92

49

93

94

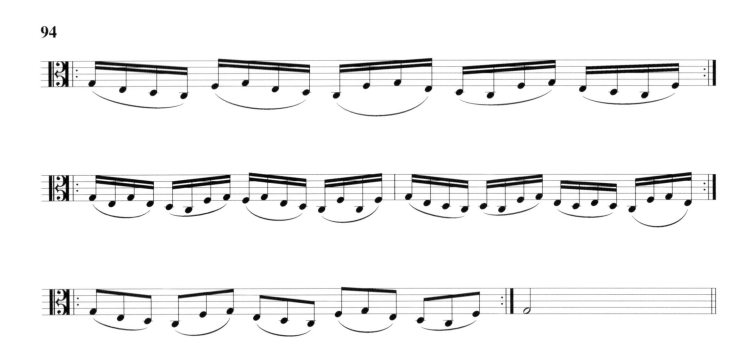

95

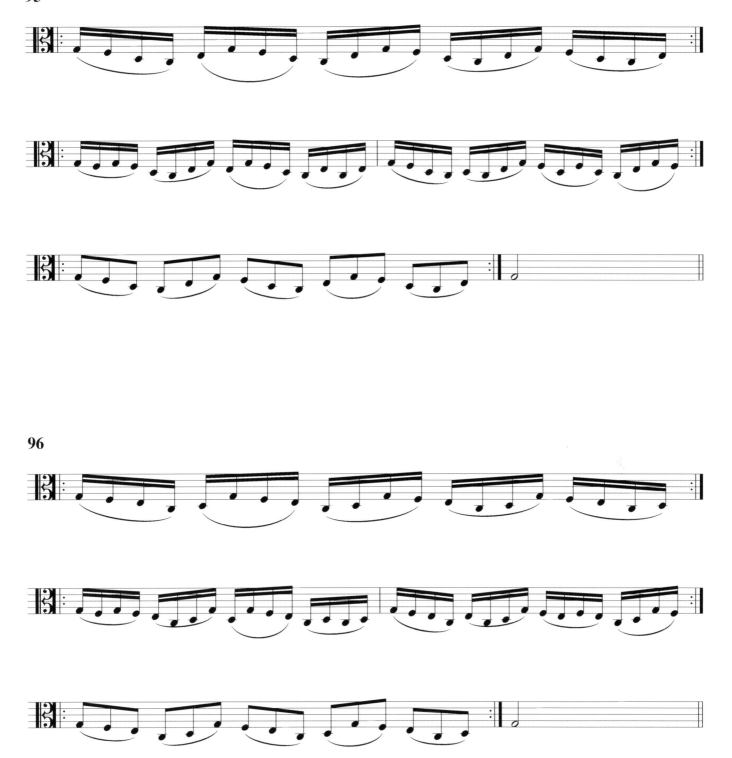

96

Eventually patterns 97-120 should be practiced in the Major key signatures of C, D, E, F, whole tones and in semi-tones. Triplets are for augmented seconds.

97

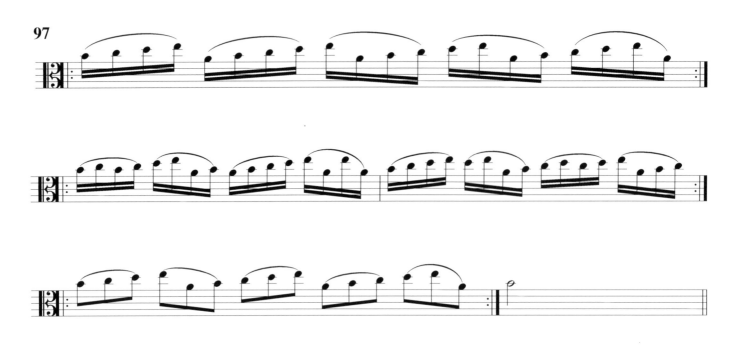

98

Always take repeats

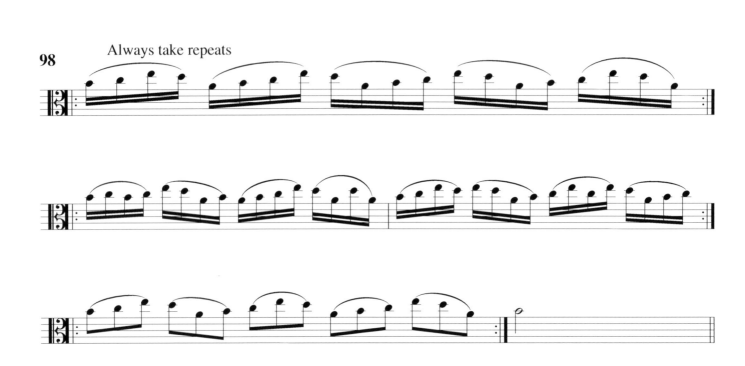

99

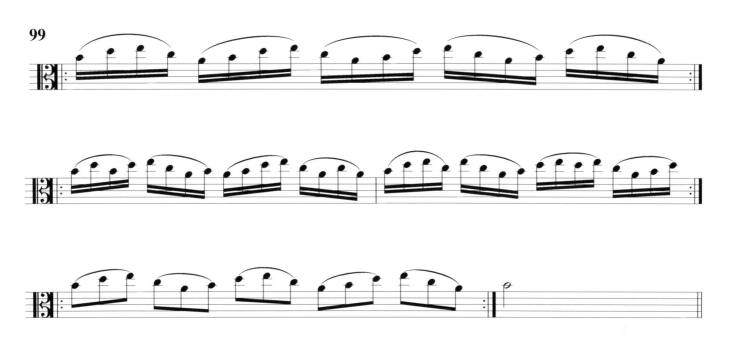

100 Focus energy in left fingers

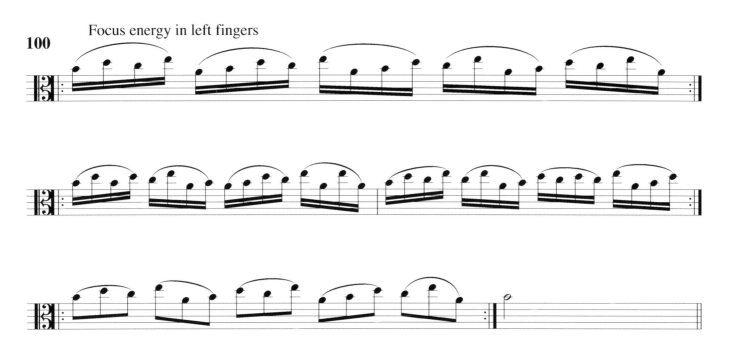

101

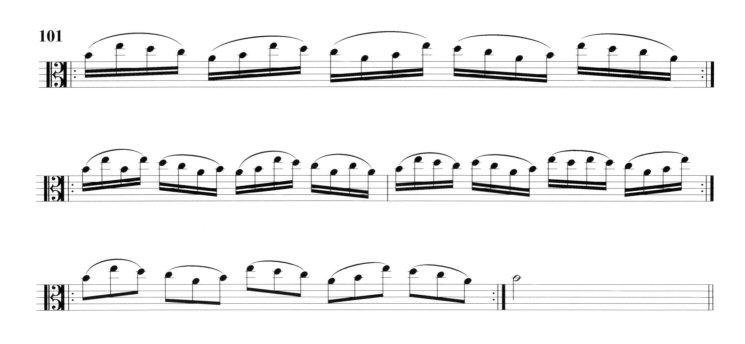

102

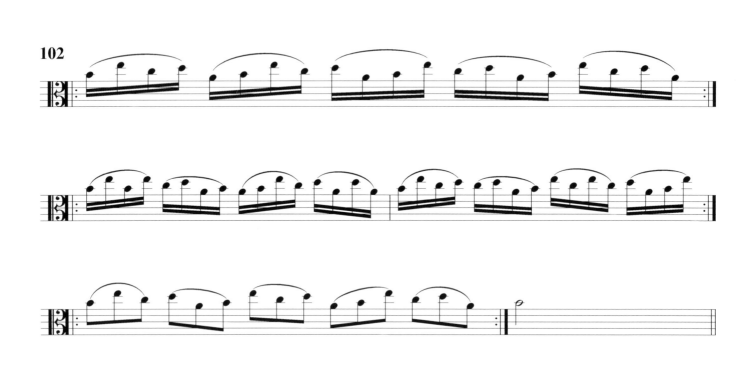

Easy attitude

103

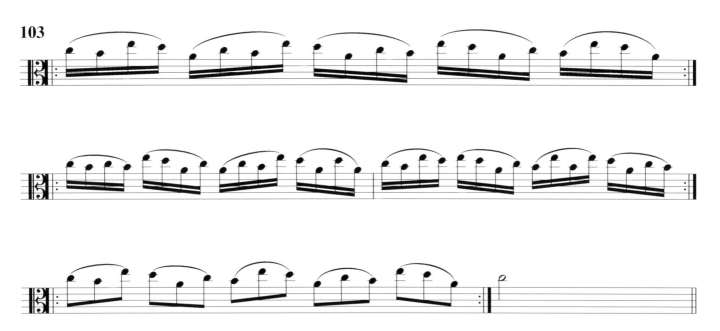

104

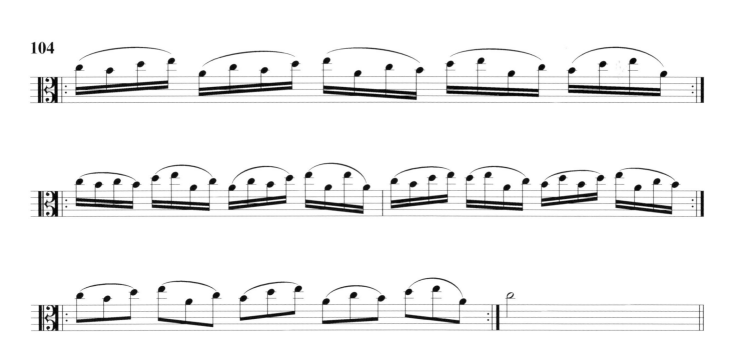

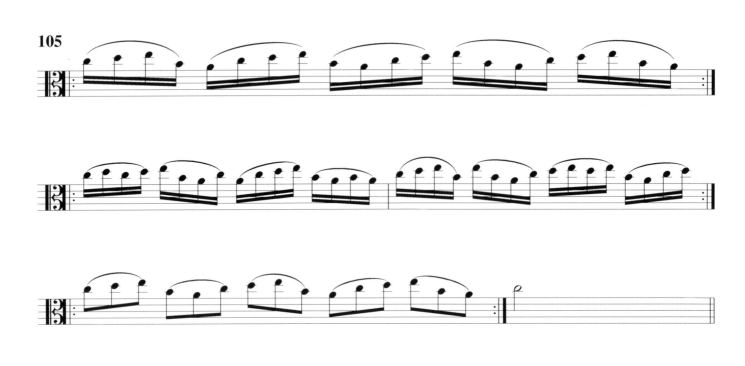

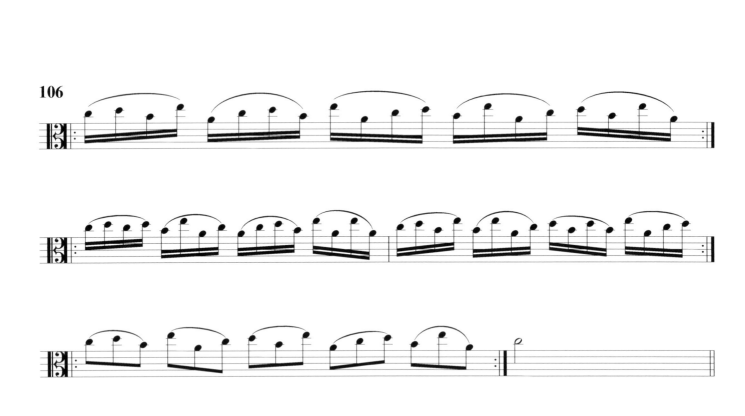

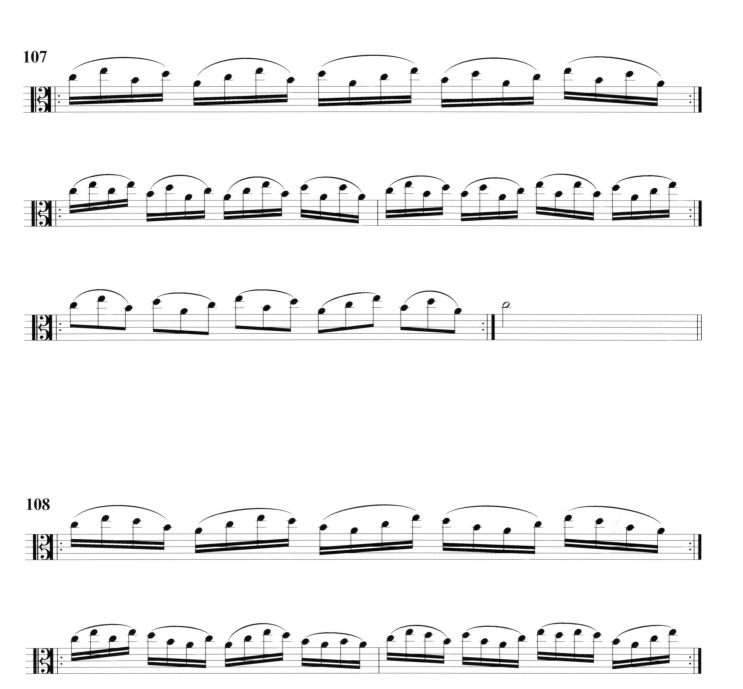

109

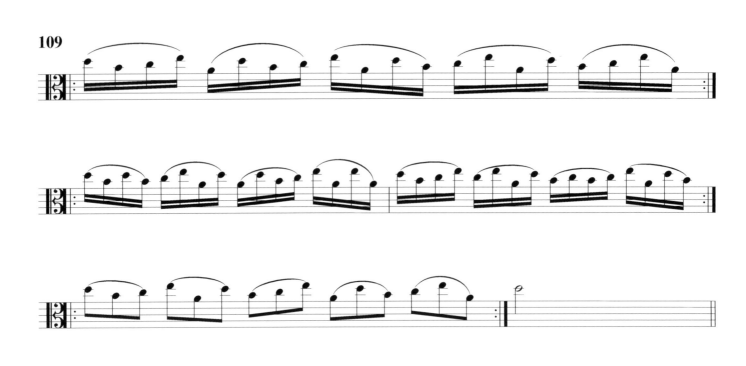

110

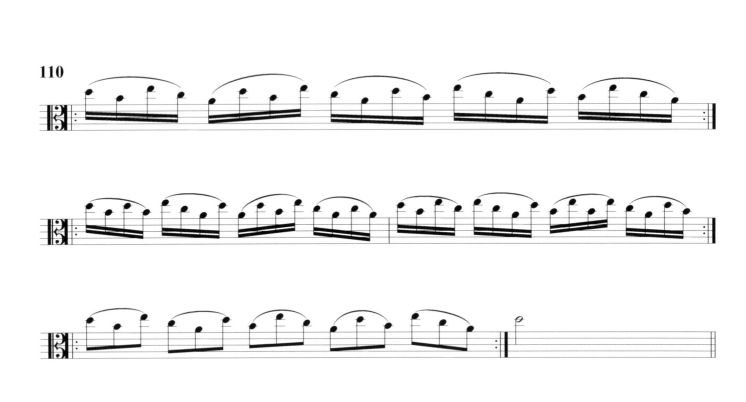

111

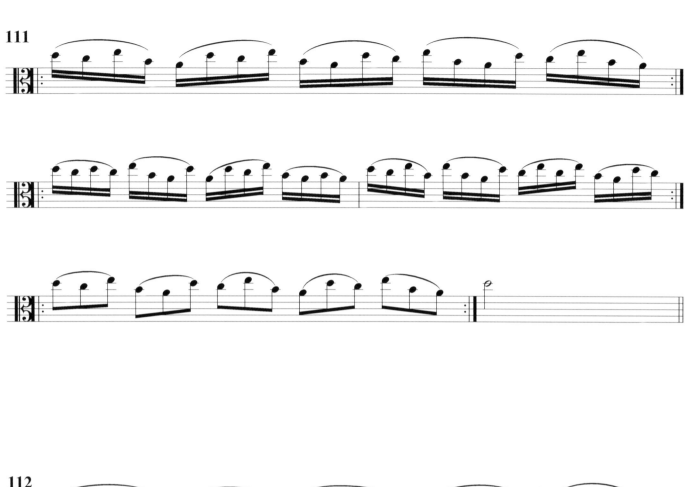

112

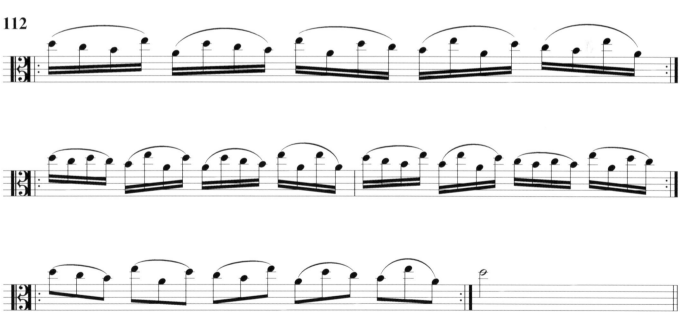

113

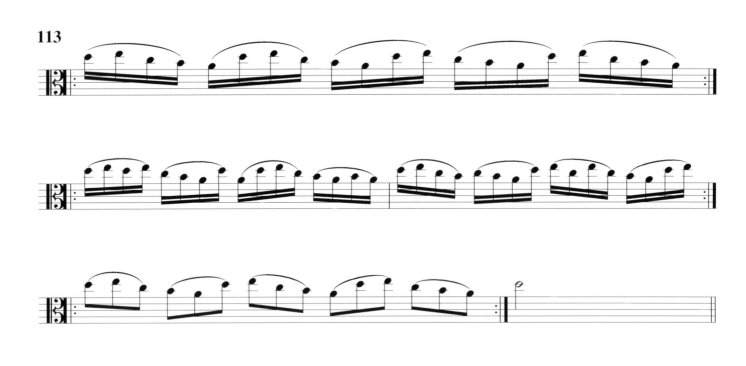

114

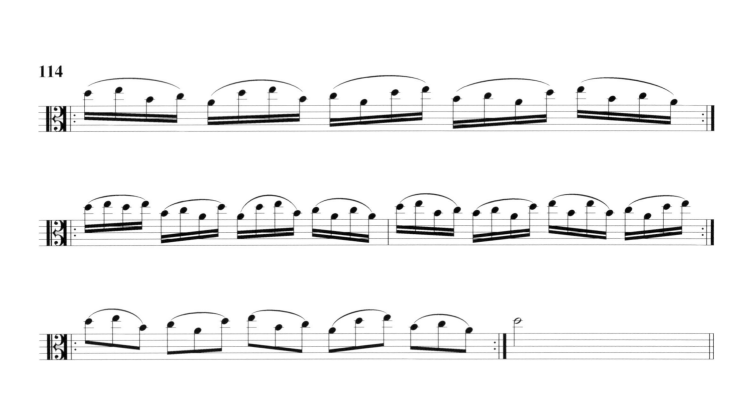

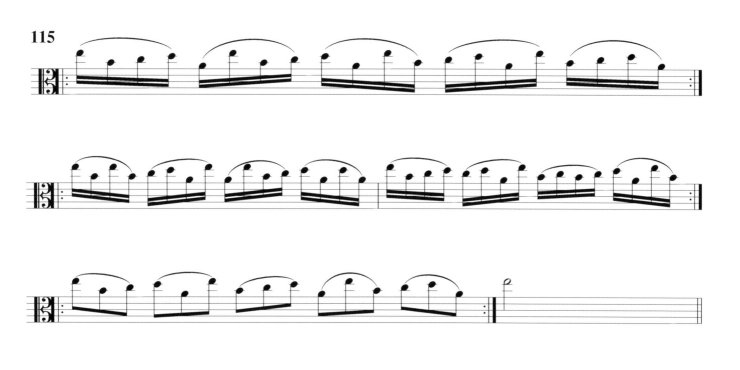

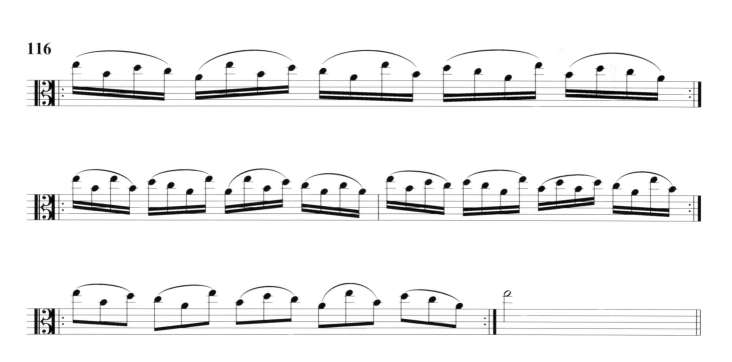

Easy attitude

117

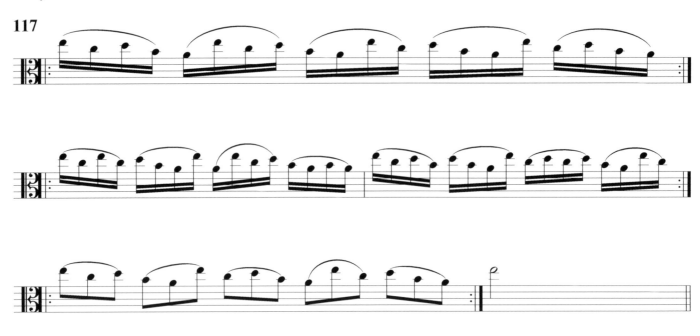

118

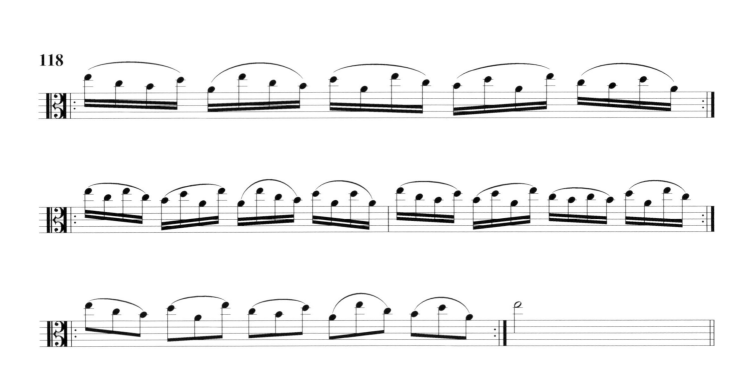

119

120

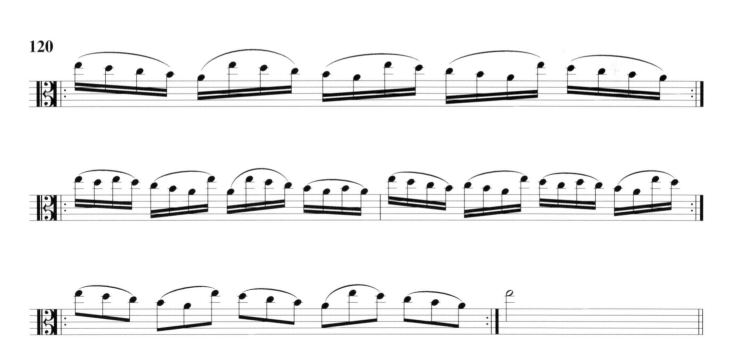

Introducing Shifting

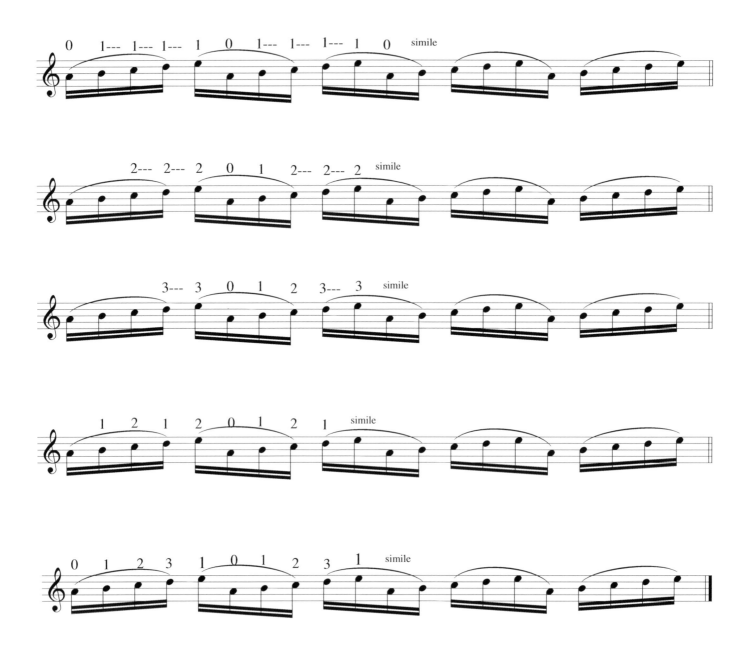

Appendix: How to Use

I. GETTING ACQUAINTED

1. Play as written (choose a "friendly" tempo; use E flat if fourth finger is weak)

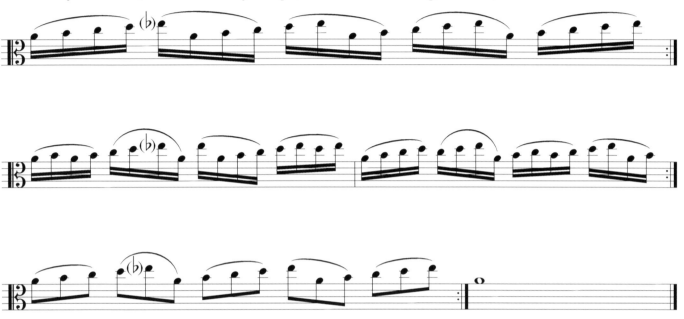

2. "The Long And Short Of It". Play in dotted rhythms (always take repeats)

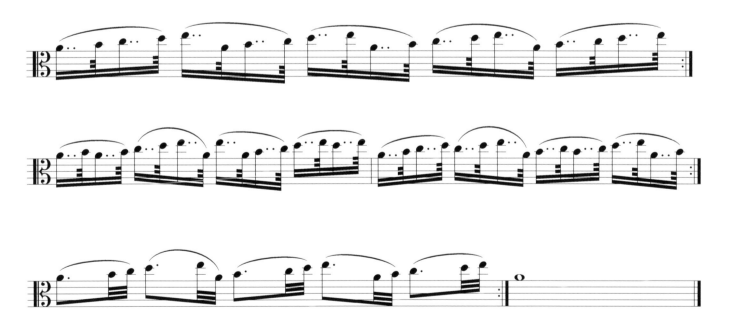

Or play short notes as grace notes

II. SPEED-READING. Training the eye.

1. "Odds and Evens": Play odd numbered groups, followed by even numbered groups.

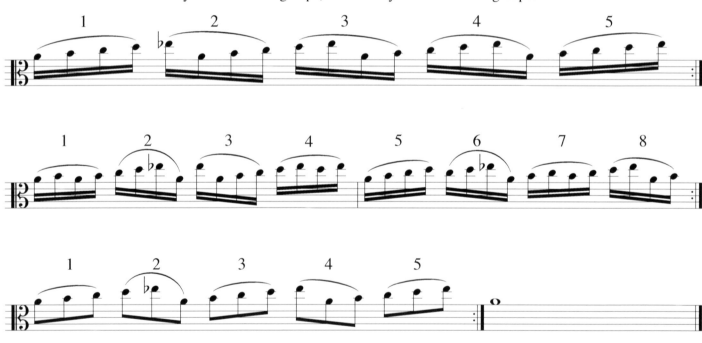

Also play other groupings, such as: 1-2, 1-3, 1-4, 1-5, 1-4, 1-3, 1-2

2. "Meet me in St. Louis". Play first group, then last group, etc...as numbered

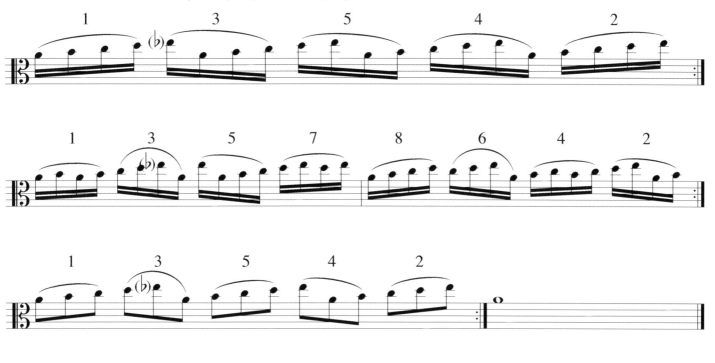

3. "Buddy System" or "The Ruler is King"
A partner holds a ruler over group being played, forcing the eye to read ahead

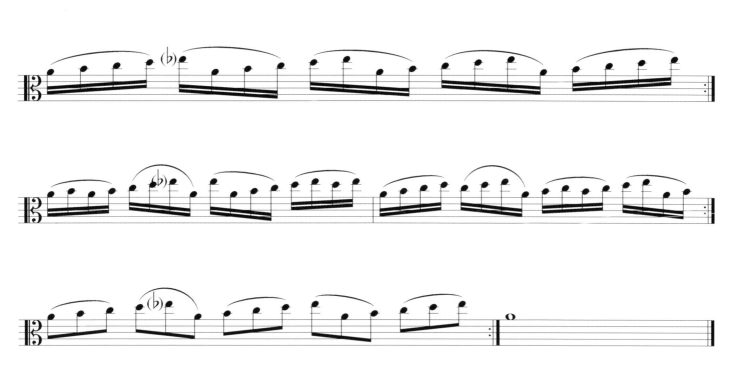

III. VELOCITY: "Speed Tracks".

1. Find fastest manageable speed. Set metronome 30% faster.
   Practice each beat plus one note.

2. Practicer in groups of 2 beats plus 1 note.

3. Continue adding beats.

4. Find *NEW* fastest manageable speed.

IV. AGILITY

While doing the above procedures keep the hand loose.
Repeating a phrase such as "loose fingers" often keeps the mind focused.
"Imaging" may help, such as "rubber fingers" or "dancing fingers".

V. FOR A CURVED AND FLEXIBLE FOURTH FINGER

1. As written, but lower the fourth finger a half-step

If the fourth finger will not curve proceed to :
   2. Practice in semi-tones

Occasionally practice without a shoulder rest--with elbow propped.
This will help the independence of fingers and a relaxed 'easy' attitude

UNIQUELY INTERESTING MUSIC!

Made in the USA